Magnetic Resonance Imaging

JON GLOVER was born in Sheffield in 1943 and was educated at the University of Leeds, where he met Jon Silkin, Ken Smith, Geoffrey Hill, Peter Redgrove, David Wright and Jeffrey Wainwright and started to help produce and edit *Stand* magazine. He spent the year 1966–7 in the United States with his wife, Elaine, who comes from near Niagara Falls. In 1968 he moved to what has since become the University of Bolton, where he is now a Research Professor. Two previous books of poetry have been published by Carcanet. He edited *The Penguin Book of First World War Prose* with Jon Silkin, and is currently researching the *Stand* and Silkin archives held at the University of Leeds and working on a biography of Jon Silkin. He is now the Managing Editor of *Stand*.

T0149076

Also by Jon Glover from Carcanet Press

Our Photographs
To the Niagara Frontier

JON GLOVER

Magnetic Resonance Imaging

CARCANET

First published in Great Britain in 2008 by
Carcanet Press Limited
Alliance House
Cross Street
Manchester M2 7AQ

A CIP catalogue record for this book is available from the British Library
ISBN 978 1 85754 967 6

The publisher acknowledges financial assistance from Arts Council England

Typeset by XL Publishing Services, Tiverton
Printed and bound in England by SRP Ltd, Exeter

For
Jeffrey Wainwright
with gratitude and the happiest of memories
of where these seem to have started.

Acknowledgements

Some of these poems have appeared in *Acumen, PN Review, Stand* and *textyle*.

Thanks are due to many people who have read and commented on some of these poems, including Jeffrey Wainwright, John Whale, Ed Larrissy, Mick Gidley, Matt Welton, Michael Schmidt, Grevel Lindop, Pat Winslow, Dorothy Nelson, Janette Jenkins, Zoe Lambert, Carole Bromley, Char March, Michael McCarthy, Julian Turner, Ella and Rodney Pybus, Nancy Shaver and John Jackson and many of my students on the MA in Creative Writing at the University of Bolton. Also to Mollie Temple, Peter Marsh and, more recently, George Holmes and Sam Johnson, who have helped to turn a difficult time into something new and enjoyable (for me, at least), and to all my colleagues at the University of Bolton.

I am very grateful to Paul Cooper, Dr Ealing and Dr Corkill, whose kind words have prompted parts of some of the poems, and to Megan Burgess, Denise Winterbottom and the other humane, student-centred staff at the Greater Manchester Centre for Neurosciences, Department of Neurology; I had a lot to learn and they are great teachers.

Special thanks to Elaine Glover and to Abigail and Rhiannon and their families for their tolerance, love and support.

Contents

Upstate Again

Seeing As

The MS Poems

Burnishing

Upstate Again

Came Back

The voices came back like wasps' nests,
like sawn timber. Such pride and dignity
rasp and chip their way into thin bits of air:

demands, contracts, bills, calendars.
Can *this* be speech? Cells, runny sweetness,
unpacked into their wasted components,

all papery dusts in the afterlife;
disputed wills, the errors of inheritance,
humming and thinking over their journeys.

Coal Bags

Flying somewhere again this summer
and, it seemed, less fearful, less attentive,
there were memories so intrusive that,
like the pressured air that sustained our lives

unsuspected pictures filled my head, bright,
scented and costumed for the part. A dog
growled, toothmarks on my skin, moist showers of
sawdust, serrated edges, heaps of coal.

I remember the coal bags, coarse, tarry
fibre between sharp, black rock and a man's
back; a muscular, shining energy
delivered thunderously to vanish in flame.

Measured in hundredweights, hods and shovels,
the slow, crushing steps to doorways,
vertebrae compressed to bursting until
they could be shrugged off like death

like transport to the upper air, settings
for diamonds, a way of bottling things
to give us warmth, to catch the light;
from the depth, pleading a price: syllables.

Bullet or Fossil

And then, as though from a stone
or whatever, I saw the bodily fluids
leaking back. Concrete soil.
Staining the undergrowth.
It's in a forest, so it's gunshots,
wildlife and photography speeding past.
I can hear it growing. For walking
thus in front of the car, you can be
dead or a memory. Look up, look
up. Pass back through your cell wall
membranes. Passing algorithms. The sums
are right as though by osmosis.
It comes to this, diaphanous, beautiful,
like the soap that cleans it down
and the ink that writes it and the
dough rising, rising, to be rolled out
and eaten. Or marble, or sheets of
gold and silver. It's skin deep only.
Like a wild garden, like what the animal
sees as it falls and leaks away round
its last bullet-hole.

Darkrooms: In the Box

Celluloid rolled up, the edges
of such tiny negative worlds
feel solid between my finger and thumb.
Into the camera, into the developer
into the printer; reels laced up.
Pictures slide over each other
and together. I'm pressing them
back into the darkroom. They're
in my finger ends and there must be
no light. Hear them. Touch
them but, again, only on the edges. Sharp.
Push them into their lightless frames.
Families, portraits, the children at all
ages, landscapes. There, and I'm touching
you, it'll be a good one, smiling;
and that, and I'm in a darkroom
touching, or sealing more film into the camera,
keep it out of the sand and sunlight,
and I'm closing it with my eyes
shut. It's all in there to be touched,
touching. Passing across the correct frame size
in the dark. An intimate exchange
from another world, like a postwar gift
to the planned, local economy of taste
of crystallised fruit through
the post from relatives in Australia.

I Thought of Pretty

Door is so much like a muscle that has lost
something dear. The dream tugging old
nerves from the back of beyond, from old
attachments. Opening to the weight of a room
made soft and tight and gummy. It's a slug
pulled in, contracted to walk on, to walk
past to the insides of worn hinges,
to the air blowing hard like the push
and pull of magnets upon my finger ends, below
my arm, under an eyelid. See it.
See it. As though the wind would pull it
from its roots, or with its last roots too,
until it all shuts again. And there,
in the garden, new lettuce leaves
shivering aside and to, aside
and closed. Brush through the weight on the far
side; so much delicacy touching
between sectors of air. Shut tight,
I thought of pretty and then you could eat it.

Wing

And now it's a petrified forest.
Crystallised wood. Pressed into coal.
Pressed into rock. I'm a tourist in
this. Imagine the process? No. Just
remember where you are with a tour guide
touching the cross-section of a tree
made stone. Heat; it's shining back. Now
it's just the light. And if you can see
through it, it weighs nothing. And you
can't take it away. So I'm back on this
coach. Organise and note the botanic cells
collected together and accounted
with our lenses shut away. Till the next
stop. And the lens adjusted for
depth of focus into the ground, as was the
sea and through anything, or invisibly
supporting our bodies as we sip
sweet fluids in the air, spelled out like
a hummingbird's wings, or a dragonfly
hiding in a wonderful calculation:
now you see it; now you don't.
Cane sugar passing on. Beaten. Beaten.

You're Gone; Like Ears

Inner ear swimming; shoals of proud
meaning flick and rebound, beyond light
and beyond hope. There, behind the eardrum,
sea surface, storm cover, untouchable
brown candles a million miles away
into the brain. So far; from Dogger Bank
to Iceland in a shimmering trice. Submarine.
Far. Tails and mouths bounce and eat one
distance under the glazed, wind-worn surface.
Brain, call it miles deep; two thousand. Call
it anything. Call.

This morning, as I left the front door,
a snake curved away under the house
as though bearing transports of
sound to move into the house's mind,
for its horror and peace. Records circling.
Read only. Spun to dust. Yes, that quiet.
Its skin's casts, like the old sounds,
disk-cases shelved away, the deafened sounds
(cash falling into place in an old phone machine –
irrecoverable, rolling downwards),
the gaunt, grey-brown words of the deaf,
blowing light and dry, so, above the sea
but listening, as ghosts, transparent
with their imagined perfect hiss.

Blemish

I'm drying a metal garden chair
after another night's rain. Paper
away the clear globes' shine
over scratchy, converging rust spots.

Bright colours gone for good
so the steel looks near
some earth colour, or tree bark,
and what's left of summer flakes

away. It's funny and worn
like blemished skin,
the urgent scab's defeat. Scars
so near to speaking out loud.

Skin to break on the edges.
Like sea spray brushing
off, to go on deeper between,
from waves, from the giant swell

of the oceans over that way. Here,
the fluff and dust of spores blowing free.
I'm waiting. It will go fine under
the snow soon. A mosquito tries its strength

as if anything soft would do. And it's
so right, its target displayed. Metal
nothing. Iron easy. Tongues and lips
suck it in. Breaking surfaces.

The snow will hardly need to try.
'Jon, you don't understand how far
everything is from here. The nearest mall,
the nearest Burger King, is an hour and

a half.' Tender. Hand over? No, that's it.
All this has to cost nothing and it's free
to the split walls between. New moles, new
crying skin punch drunk to a silent, dry freeze.

Dare Like Dead

Glass door. Deliberately,
you hoax. And a painted frame
like a landscape or portrait
turned inside out, like a sock,
a sleeve with its dust and
old moisture there to see. So
that's what you see again,
the posts and lock
socket, the joints and wood
shaped vision of the other side.
Other, to so nearly slam your face
into. It's not there and not there.
It's there, or then, for table settings
with no diners, hearth, coal scuttle.
It's alert and firm and untaught. Taut.
Unheeded. Flowers in a frame.
Skinned, skimmed to the wall. Uncoated.
And still old heart valves, aggregations
of what you've meant, clamming up the walls,
and there the transparent shape
beckoning; to walk towards; past
the painted frames; dare like dead.

Driving Down

Driving down the river track –
it was a road on the map
at least – and on one side
a steep edge into the forest

and no way back, since the tires
wouldn't grip, and forwards so
near to sliding over. On the map
a single simple track due north.

And all this weight works round
for itself like a compass slithering
round to whatever truth it leaves
or can put up with. The motor rotates

its skull in old oil and chains. If it
could face it. If it could see
its face and work it. And, lovely gravity,
so many lines of force, scattered

(do you remember the iron filings spread
on paper? Do you need all that under
your fingers? Grinding, dusty, spun silk?
That, so.) The better road is touching (tongue –

tap, tap) and smirking. There now. There now. Silk
worm. Tumbling like a strange heavy cocoon
unwinding from the boiler, unravelling
from the rattling inner body weight.

The Beautiful Machines

Moving things in, moving things:
you could talk about machines for living
but it's not that; not at all what brings
gadgets and cups and saucers and picture frames
waiting to be filled and oiled and smoothed
and piled in front of the old ones.

It's here, and lost, behind a new mismatched
coffee set, between five table lamps,
in front of a torn, stained landscape painting.

There's a view, quite spectacular, from behind those
trees, and that patch of bent grass may have held
a sleeping deer. And here's a catalogue
of metal-working tools from 1907 – but we don't
make those things any more – though they are now
quite beautiful; no, don't need them, and if
we set up that sharpener it would be so precise
you could shave with the chisels and the motor
would make the house shake and hum; so, wait
for now; but that screw and that wood-vise
could set things going, again, quite beautifully, and here's
another room waiting to be shaped and filled
and become something that's never there again.

More Trash

Put the trash out (like a freed cat, to walk
its own ways), recycling or the furnace
or the landfill, all despicable fuels,
poisonous adjustments to the here and now

and love. Put it as though it's books to be
read for unintended stories, for wild
detachable fictions, desperate echoes
in the oncology lab. It's the words

I can't be bothered with, fluttering through
the tip, and remember, the other bits
we don't want, it's art and so valuable
and we horde it and frame it and give it

names. So there, so get on with it, trash
I said, awaiting the old disposal
company, this roadside line-up, after
orders and fulfilment, to be inhaled

and stroked like a new fragrance (scratch and sniff):
the grammar's rolling deeper and mutating;
pet it, put it to bed (feed a cold and
starve a fever), the squeezed milk of human

kindness, self-expression coming back to
get you and there's no help, no earthly help.

Risk

Such as crying, such as grooming a horse
that seems intent on its own directions:
the height of its breath, the muscles beyond

concentration, beyond the death. In a
dark stable, dry walls lined with leather and
blankets, it's waiting to emerge, its turn

unbuckled, its love bouncing from the walls
and to the door like a shelled pea from my
thumb and fingers; and the floor shining

from the brush and comb and water. Out there
the light so far away, it's cross; moving
away to a jump, momentarily.

It's in the middle of a bridge, a tear,
a value, splitting hairs, a parting. What's
lamented is all that's present. Gifted.

Site

'The site of a battle between Schoharie
militia, Indians and Tories in
1783.' It's forest now.
And then? Hopeless bribery from unloved

worlds; commanding into science towards
gunshots and poison. Working the trees, back
to back. No echoes. No news. Bandaged for

months to slide through the trees again. Blanked out.
It's all too prickly. Stinking uniforms.
I can only think of the enormous
pleasure of solitude. For anyone,

what would it have been worth? For food? For crops?
For whatever force allowed the spring again?
I can hear a power saw and a hunter's pleasurable gun.

Would that have scared the lot away if they
could have heard? Dead meat, the maps rolled up, ships
stocked up with corn. Soldiers file through a long,
covered bridge as though to be flattened, ironed

out; white clothes washed and smoothed to make our
bodies and landscapes holy. Back to the
port. It might as well go. Everything has to go.

Snakes Again

Three snakes under the doorway today.
Between the stone steps. And the same
stone colours, and a gash into the dark.
As such, I watched for as long as it took.

Boo. Giant sawcut through the windows and
floors. Leasing leaks through the broody
cellars to the Ice Age before, and the
glacier scrapes. Down and along, fervent

dragging toothmarks. Socket. Stone-cast
metabolism. Something's cold tongue.
A photograph if I want it. But it's
somewhere in my head, slumming. Head over

heels. Tread water. The glacier might retch
in its sleep, so slowly. And if the
jetstream twisted over this way to
move these rocks again? And if the snow?

Crouching overwards to the least spent warmth;
slimy crystals. There they are again,
playing at justice above the water table
under the concrete, under the palm of my
hand, under the flat light. Thoughtless. Easy.

Themselves Dry

Then clouds sucking themselves dry.
And the wind rising like a giant mirror
in my ears. You can't hear it. You can't
hear it. And, like desire, into thin air.

Priceless. Or priceless words floating
down; parachuting to become
stretched waterlilies, or anything afloat,
and the bodies hanging beneath,

not gardening, but digging the water.
And above, the soundless blossom –
look up to its veins, down to the earthy
surface. And I'm leaning, dizzying

down through the water. Drops to the touch,
whatever you say, like some mercury, soft metal,
and scatter behind the mirror. Reflects; and so perhaps
it's as clear as can be and all that can be.

Walking, Not Waking

Waking to white lightning
it's hard to think it doesn't
know what it's about. It's creaking
overhead and squeezing the
electric clouds. For lifelike
and nervy water. Spitting such.
And some of the white is flickering
so close it doesn't need thunder
to touch ground. I'm not trying
to sleep now. Beside bent
trees the dogs and deer will scare
and not remember. It can hardly
wait to die out. It's moving
through the valley and licking
the air clean like the snake's
tongue. I'm turning over again
for more sleep. The phone
blinks. In the night, I suppose
I'm looking for fear. And the
electric company waiting for
3 a.m. calls, 'The light's gone.
Trees out of the ground.'
The walls are white again
from the colourless dry sparks
ahead. And I'll not sleep
now till dawn. I'm nursing it.
Like something to be angry about.
In a white pillow, static
crystalline stuff clipped soullessly
into science.

Way Through

For Nancy and Jackson

Two deer crossed the road ahead. Simply a
hard interval in their forest. Random
dangers, like most of the others. So, brake

gently. They're gone. Their door shuts. Now, as if
sad, push to the speed limit again. The
car smells of rust and gas. Wet carpets. Ride

on, into sudden thunder and rain that
crackles sure and quick like a stone wall's step
collapsing as I climb over it. Storm

air to be stroked; it's under my feet. In
my ears. Lichen, upside down, brushing my
cheek; and my skin's weighted and sharp as a

carving knife. It's edgy though. It knows what's
pliable, what's a path, what suffices.
How could you go through it like they do still?

Olana

To allow for a way to see what's there.
To make it sure to be a view of the sublime
from a stone-built house on a hilltop
across the Hudson from picture-distant
hills. Or mountains, if you want them
so much as enticing; stand off, stand back:
memories of such a European eastward land.
Dull surfaces. That's what I remember.
Perhaps dusty and worn but also there as
another style – made and preserved
without glass, without polish.
Snapped out of grainy rock,
reflecting not much, not shined up,
but set like old brain cells in some ancient
preservation in Egypt, an afterlife for
all of us, imaginary riches in some
democratic paints. Outside, inside;
there as any other substance to be cut
and pasted under the mountain tops,
between the trees, quite aside from any
crushing wind or bright dawn. That's enough
to contend with. I'm not bothering now.
Let it blend. Let the stencil-work fade.
This is already its own orientalist.

Seeing As

Something Like

A thin, low fog this morning
with peaks and valleys drifting quickly,
though there seems no wind, and
the sun offering itself white
and silver every few minutes.
From an airplane – there's one,
invisible – flying low, it must
look like cross-stitch on a soft,
white ground, with the tops of trees
and houses needling through
and then submerging, unpicked
threads, as the fog thickens.

A lament, a memory, a cry,
frail portraits raised aloft for
a second or two, to be seen
and admired and passed over
and done again; the sizzling, white,
weightless flesh, folding and unfolding,
picking out its way
to ecstasy quite undefined.

Ancient Lost Poems

As though the pipe-work was there
or not there, plumbing, if you will,
for something like a decorated language
that starts with red flowers all over
but it's far away under the brick
or flesh, again, if you will,
and over it all, the patterned
clothwork, the bright metaphoric
patches hiding some leaden shrouds
of messages put to rest. Over it all,
epigrams, roses, tomb-work,
stitches, in time; standing for
something erotic or loved in the
sunshine, matching words swallowed
down, cleverly needled over sullen
lost languages. Fitting, so fitted,
to form a glowing surface. Love,
for now, labelled for size, words dye-fast.

Flying The

For Lorna Tracy

'Hello, little bird.' The thing flew
off on a first try across the pool
learning to catch the mosquitoes.
And those words, surrounding
the hollow pipes like a death–
suit, covering the hidden chart
from here to South Africa. Clothing
for the touchless flickering muscles.
Funny-bone, wish-bone, heart attack; or
a mask sucked on tight to preserve the space
between us and the consuming flight.
A dry eat; in and through and through.
Mapping into droplet existence.
Discolonialised uniform. Words,
a dark suit for the unlearned.

Oh, Crying This

For Ken Smith

Oh, crying this, like falling light today,
is rain, so loud I do not love; streams on,
parading far past stones and moss to fly

a sound. Urgent valves prised open, fine sun
spins through veins and hair lines, eyes' gentle fright
turns out, a forest of bright stings, a gun

to shoot such fat platelets, bugs flying light
through the heart. It's thumping, as finely blown,
and drives through crumbling mortar's skinless tight

fraction of joy, of heat and dread and upwards
back somewhere to muscles' eked out dreadful
nerveless thrust. To red nerve endings, and woods:

final pitch of tense and darkening eye
as though the roots could curl back, smile with rage.

The Sun Rocking

For Alice Loy

It's all so much history.
The sun rocked over. Yes, that's
what I mean – rocking, or swinging
like a baby's first love affair
with gravity in the park swing –
beside myself, beside what can
stay for that fixed moment in the
air but not slip to the ground
and rock down and up to see
the sky and again not slip
and look and back like the light
shut and open. Like breath
on a lens to evaporate, clean
gone, like tears, like milk,
balanced for now and then.
For the shutter. And for the next
story. A snapped tree
that sunlight claims.

Caen

Surveyed from far below the walls, at night,
its weight seems resting on its tombs and dross
of festering sores and anger. So contrite
for years of dominance, and painful loss
it offers facts and history, easy done,
to tourists making sense of who lived here
and why we should pay cash to sight a gun
fired with straw and tallow, against such fear
as we might think was known before the maps
and measures set it out, the English much
too hated to be known and counted, weighed
as brochures now describe the walls' high caps
restored to shine with postcards' coloured touch
that pleats aesthetics into what's decayed.

Caen and York

For Jennifer Kilgore

Below the walls of a conqueror's castle
I'm in a hotel, pink and ugly blue
walls, cold bathroom, Ouest-France, no view; hassle
to make a phone call home. One of a few
who may be worrying about a tower
in York where history scrawls its textual land
to be written on to what will fill our hour
of guilt or reconstruction, stone unmanned,
to fight through this old, planned and guarded muck
to tour these sites and sleep and relish war
as though we'd beaten that and now can shuck
the guards and gloves from hands content with law.
Imagine a well up there. En suite, fast
in rock, shit, blood, cold wounding: fleet forecast.

Arms

It's work and our dignity in labour;
it's the market to offer the spare parts
for constitutions and liberation and territorial
integrity. Reverential slips of

the tongue, bloody insults, (words are free);
a whole descriptive paradise where innocence
comes into the bargain beneath missiles'
guided flight. That's what you want? A passion

like this in promissory notes? Death quite
clear and accountable coming from the
open sky to be just what they deserved,
or we, or you, just as in some other

story, some fiction or art where the words
must make a mark and do the dirty deed
for some author or authority? And
they're all there in the factory up the road,

waiting shipment, waiting delivery;
the words that make the whole war and nothing
but the war. And by trying to make sense,
we've asked for it, and put it in writing.

Button Box

For Pat Winslow

Almost sacred. A collection jilted
from some heaven, or an island
lined with tusks and whalebone.
Seafarers just in black and white.
An economy in slivers of shell,
mother of pearl, dull plastic. Rustling
as the lid twists off. And like a bank
with coins set out for you to plunge
your fingers into, to ruffle through,
to warm, the buttons were there so deep
and invaluable because they were
for no other use. Saving for the blitz?
For the dead? From the dead? For brave
cut out clothes, cold dolls? Something
female and unfathomable? For repairs
that might hold us together, like a shirt
to be made respectable again. Shut in,
shut down. Like the breathless milk teeth
stored at the back of a bedroom drawer.

Duty Free

They say the Russian stocks of nuclear junk
are leaking west into the wrong hands.
A few grams found at a German airport
(did it set off a routine alarm like the keys
and change in my pocket?) and the balance
of power tilts even further from its old
textbook presentation. The game's got different
rules now and they aren't written down. And so,
my attention shifts, you see: there's the forest
and the sound of some distant machines.
The sky, for once, is perfect blue. Written,
written so that one might weep for what goes on
in the imagination, for what's allowed,
what the words can do without prompting.
Like the birdsong that's still out there,
that just has to mean something, doesn't it?
We've been trying to record it for years,
to turn it into music, to type it
phonetically in the identification handbooks.
So that you'll know what it is that's singing
and that it's beautiful and that it's back
next year and you'll know where to find it.

The Function of Dreams

It was as good as climbing a hill, as though
(as though), frightened by boundaries, by all
the wars (stuff) about to be manifest
from the distant side. So that's it: distant,

the aggregations of splendour unexplained,
plaintive, translucent castles on the plain
just so, where you are lost, evaporating
alone on the far side. After, after –

fill it in with sticks, stones, cotton waste and
spit; cuckoo spit, grubby apparitions
(as though) a comic stand-in, stealing and
skewing and vain. Such strife and forgetting.

Instruments

Between how things are seen
and touched. Between. Scuffling
like layers of air from north and south
for a smell of this. The air

again breaking waves, breaking
trees. Thumped through a cylinder
block and squirted into these roadside leaves.
Cylinder-head snuffling and breathing for

anything that smells good. Now backing,
hurtling down the road. Smells at
the seams of clothing. Dogs clasping
the old pheromones and laughing. Into

the shed of bent iron and piping.
Structures repeating themselves and rolling
down the machined hot exhaust pipes
for all they're worth. The richest

staining oils. Waste metals. Waste colours.
Crank that bright rainbow. It's
raining so hard it'll carry the metal away.
Backing away. So like rain.

So like clouds licking through the valleys
and hillsides. As if they cared for the
shape of things, for the surfaces of bodies.
Photos of pearl corpses; moths lapping white.

Postwar

I cannot think how this has happened
apart from – there is the rushing sound
of a car approaching fast – it's so true

to itself, like a comet's tail, like glossy
oils of freedom and purchase. And there, perhaps
(no need), other machines arrayed in silence,

the black oils sucking their bearings;
waiting, wakeful but inward (at midnight)
such as a dentist's drill, the hydraulic rams

and presses, alone between the shifts. In
space, bright and starred, and sleeker than
polished teeth, than crowns, it's our framework of

ideas in a world of plenty, postwar;
it's our molten casting of love and we're
working, loss over loss, on its halo.

The Study Floor

My father had Eddington, Jeans and Hoyle,
for the common reader. They were piled
along with letters, Freud, Jung and *A Handbook
on Hanging*. A sort of Brains' Trust on the
floor, the shelves, spare chairs; placed. Think of
writing about that all before rockets
and measuring radio waves from other
galaxies. Think of writing. Or polishing
the instruments to grind a mirror or a
lens. To see the moon you needed
the skill of a jeweller; jeweller's rouge,
moon dust. What will the surface be like?
Like canals, like the giant cathedrals
of our own sea floor. Like metaphors
on paper that just had to be written,
and thus, unquestionable, as you see.
Shadows silently available
at the twist of a cog. (Remember queuing
for the new Biro? And Teach Yourself.)
Telescopes, microscopes engineered for
the monarchy. Polite timepieces of
Greenwich, there to read about on the study's
tacked felt and floorboards; a surface, spotted
with knowledge, like a distant planet
flattened on the sky, to be reached, walked over,
through dust, quiet voices, papery secrets.
And, just so unattainable, as I
turned past the simple formulae of light
years, to the conclusions: 'If we could journey
and see ourselves, but it will not be in
our lifetime.' So, write about it. Turn the
pages. Polish the style. And what did you
take away with you? Sick. Calculating
the drop? The interpretation of dreams?
Dust and mildew; forcible grinding through
the wars to this day? Hush. With your face curved
into it. The smell of what it will be.

Watch on Deck

For Elaine

Look down between the quayside
and the side of the ship – two worlds
rotating slowly and opening and closing
like eyelids over the sea and the scum
and orange peel and plastic and weed.
Motes. Cast off; drift apart. The massive walls open.
It's the sky and then nothing; it's twisting foam
and then perfect, straight wake. It's
hull down and silence apart from throbbing
engines, the never quite repeated judder
of the bow against new waves; pattern
and no pattern. It's there, calling long distance:
How are you? How was the journey? (Digits,
waves, reflections, decoders, satellites
and you might be in the next room.) Tonnage,
transport sliding away over the surface
of the earth like continental drift. Do you know
where it's going? What it feels like?
The fuel bills? The phone bills? The weighty
dictionaries that account for what we've said
so long after the event? So long. See you.
The weather's good here, on the deck,
on the tarmac, in the saloon, wherever.
Precious messages, like a ship in a bottle;
like dolls and model aircraft we hadn't the heart
to give away. Cast off. Cast away. Truly
like knots, like knitting, like moorings and all
the attempts to take up unfinished embroidery.
Keep watch. It's all you can do, I think.

The MS Poems

Back to the Diagnosis

Attending. Attentive. I was in an ordered group.
I'm not sure if I felt it was a competition
although, as I recall it now, it did seem like
a slow race, or waiting to fall off a bicycle too high
or too shiny (surely, not for me). Or for a language
examination for which I'd forgotten the name
of the country, or whether it was ancient or modern,
or to prepare for use with some unpredictable future
aliens. Soon it became a test to choose the door
to open along the corridor, the door for me,
and there you have it. And that's what I did. Since I won
that one. The nice man asked me in to stand on one leg
and stand on the other. To walk with one foot exactly
in front of the other ('I bet you've not done that
since the school playground') although I don't ever remember
such an act in my childhood, so familiar as part
of his routine chat, but I do remember falling over
and over then, lonely, like on this exciting new day that,
as he said, had nothing unpleasant or undignified.
So I thanked him when he asked me if I knew anything
about messages that didn't get through. And I knew the
answer. So I thanked him again. For the verbs that didn't
agree, the ball that dropped short, for historic physics firing
up the electro-magnetic attraction with pulses that
got more and more tired of the race. 'Try it again, and raise
your arms. Try it again and push my hands. Try it again
and tell me what you can feel on either side of your
face, or in this ear or that, or in this eye or that. And then
we'll know. So that's that then.' And out to the corridor
and the waiting room and the files and the right time.

Cells

Cells: they make you up in botany
or any other living science. Human
biology. Listen to it. Stretch
and cut and pin back to make
the deepest interior a visible surface,
a joint, a leaking edge. Could I
have seen that in a paper cut,
a grazed knee? Childhood
journeys to unfelt centres,
the hot cellular structures disallowed;
no pictures or diagrams where you're
going. Explain 'Kiss it better'.
I think not. Touch, dissect, record.
Good enough. Maps and charts, coloured
cross-sections: the clear instructions
to keep things as they are. I still love maps.
They smell clean and special on your skin
and unfold awkwardly like sticking plaster.

My Mother's Microscope

'So, you see, the paper and printing isn't
all that is to be seen. It's not that what's there
isn't there, if you see what I mean; it's just
that in a lab you have to look closer.'

I remember the first time I saw a printed
letter (say 'a'), or pencil line (say 'figure'),
yes, it could mean a 'number' or a drawn 'body',
through her microscope. Choices. Graphite and

clay powders scratched behind the pitted surface
and heaped against scattered timber fibres –
this, the breakdown of paper into china glaze
and wood, the precious place of records, pictures

and maths. Write it first so it comes good.
That's where your pen and ink go: to pieces.

Sucking a Pencil

For Rodney and Ella Pybus

Through another lesson on the shape of
continents, the drifts, the patterns that no one
understood, I was stuck in my mind's eye
(find that I thought) with the jigsaw joints in

the skull my brother had bought in his first year
at Guy's and left neatly on the mantelpiece
over the fire, of course, just to keep it
warm to the touch. The plates jiggled slightly.

It was hard not to squeeze my head to see
if its shapes would move, however slightly,
like a cracked schoolroom globe to be laughed at.
Sockets. Keep chewing through the earth's surface

scripts. Coloured pencils now filling in a
diagram of the Rosetta Stone. Compare
and label. Explain and discuss. Can you want
it? Where might it be put away and stored

for when the similarities might skin
over as love? To cover the hollow,
cleaned out space for formulae of knowledge
awaiting nervous desire. Suck it in,

suck what you write with, to hold in brain cells
and fibres. There, that word again, painted
into your skull, or mine, to be electrified
and spat down the axons or faultlines,

any picture here, any picture there;
dictionaries, vocabulary practice
or geography so, a paradise
erupting out at the sea bottom,

rough scabs at the tectonic plates' edges,
down there and hurting for all to see.
So now, years later, we know what goes on. Drift.
Close your eyes, taste the pencil, see inside.

Pens Unpurchased

Another lost poem, you see.
Behind a wall? Wallpaper?
Pocketed into sand or cement,
the floor shuts down, written over,
hidden secret prize below an
easy fountain pen script. Sucked inks.
Taps into gravity's semi–
detached talk with absolute zero.
Warm? Huh. Soul's in there.
Through bodies flying round into
the after-life. Atoms falling out to a
plain existence. Royal blue
washable territories to be filed,
flat surface upon flat surface,
an act in the dead of night.
You see the sticky plaster
modelling over some dry plain, buffaloes'
instinct, wide, wide. Or over the tundra,
lights out, cold out. Filed down, as
indeed white finger nails might be,
positing, posturing as labels for
hot and cold. Taps some more.
And cold, of course. Cut off. Unpainted.
The bitten, chewed, guilty dusts
of someone's art form held in the hand.

Make Over

Lips, eyelids, crying for words.
Dictionaries flickering over;
splat. Flute, sucked music reeds
crystal muck, mucus kissed
ways into meaning, void
and breath – lick, you pliant
cushions of beauty, décor
stuck together and over with colour
gutted from a whale's chemicals five
miles deep and harpooned pricked
lungs. Fright. You won't love. You won't
count. You won't root through a slick
alphabet of slime to what you want.

Picture It as if from a Cave

Waiting to be seen. I like it thus. In
the dark, as a fantasy without a name.
Nervy. Cord. Chord. The sound of metal piano
strings stretched out for tons of pleasure yet to come.

Believe the picture's there on a rocky surface,
awaiting your very own prescription,
so it looks as if its historic sense
makes sense for you at its new ground level.

Stamp on it. In your dreams. Print. A picture,
perhaps, of random hits. If you can hold
on long enough, the protons and quarks might
come round again and display a summer's day,

a face, an eyelid closing and opening –
smash again, and there you have it:
the smell of electricity at a
fairground, dodgem cars with sparking contacts,

that message from above to look where
you're going. The circuit boards easily
packed in a truck, for the next waste-ground stop.
Remember those flash-bulbs that melted down

into the untouchable, bubbled shapes
of injured eyeballs. All to gain the worth
of an image of perfect resolution.
Leave it. Tone it down. It's getting dangerous.

Like CERN

Attacking the immune, a system
it might seem, with relish. Go on,
you love the barrier, the build-up
the horse-trading through atomic walls.

Even if it's an image too good
to last. The ground water, the water
table, the space for drink and vomit
leaking into posterity. I could stand back

amazed to hear that the blood-brain curtain,
that's silently offered safety for years
has let the smash seep through. But talk like that
seems crass. You can't really have it perfect

in your head. For now, atoms are fed up
with their cool body-image, and clustered
happy to reform, they offer another
explanation that lets you feel it's someone's

fault. Mine, I'm sure. Left-over plates. To dine
on transparencies. Lick it up. Wash it
clean. I don't want any reminders. Surface
patterns? Not much left. Perhaps the deeper

circuits want a signature to cherish.
It's so nice up here. Offer them some hope?
Try blotting paper soaking up your name,
that mirror-written record of your will,

going backwards as it might, manifest
destiny, an acceleration screeched
into reverse, all there as if someplace
else, touched by a quill pen, some moveable

type, paper, skin, with a verdict stuck in
the old simple minerals. Unmoved. It's
only working for itself. Trash it. Blind
down there. Soaked silently. Wasn't written.

CERN: Frontiers, Grave-Diggers

Like the infinitely splitting particles, circling
to destruction between Switzerland and France.
Why bother with them? It seems I'm digging
them out for the sake of it. Sick. Really sick.

It's as if particles from wartime corpses
might have seeped home in the soil from Verdun,
to either side, pining for an explanation,
or a chance to rest, or to forget what

they once were by becoming quite invisible.
Does anything verbal stack up the voltage
for such bright light? It could be a holding
charge, static, while waiting to see if the

rotting matter can be read out loud
in the form of a script to make a plea,
or warm an electric coil to switch off
the guilt, since you're not immune from that now.

Press. Pass it on. It works so long as you
can't see it. Close your eyes and listen
to the document in your head. There now.
Buy. It trickles through in no time at all.

Reformation

Perhaps the accelerator is built
like a giant pen to scribble out some
predestined, unarguable word under
Calvin's city. I wonder if those speeding

fragments are flicking through my brain right now
with their own scripture. So much for authority.
Try it, fine it, sentence it. If only
you could put it down for future reference.

Take pictures or drugs. Make your choice,
or let it go. Go. It's mining under
city streets, hills, streams. Splatter
into any old shape the magnetic

tunnels have prepared. The site
of something called a reformation.
I hardly think it makes sense enough
to worry about. Clean it up for

the visitors' sake. So, go on then.
Roll up. Pay for it. It's the least
you can do. Offer this: coins sliding
down a fairground trick, worn-smooth,

cash-winning table. Try this sweet attraction:
quiet airplanes circling and waiting to land
on soft grass (as if they could). Pay with this:
plastic, banked invisible assets.

A Shared Vision

For John Barnard

Illness gives you a way of seeing things.
Museum or surgery? The stuff has
to work. Polished, dovetail jointed drawers
of surgical instruments keep things tidy.
Like clothes perhaps, or papers; spices for

cooking or preserving. I am amused
to think of Keats crossing St Thomas's
Street early to be well positioned in
the dissecting theatre for a good view
into a flapping, pinned back, muscular

stench; looking down, into a play on words,
through the audience, rows of heads, laughing
or swallowing hard, onto the table,
the bucket, the saw, the demonstration
of what's inside, waiting to fall apart.

Knives, shutters, light, boxes. Moving backwards
and forwards, in and out of the known world.
Pack it into a pin-hole camera,
an amphitheatre, a telescope, or
a walk-in camera obscura.

So you can pass it round, share the print, frame
today's insight, whatever you can get
into, bring it up for analysis.
Sick. Like being seasick to order. Bowls.
And there they were, sections of spinal cords,

tinted and labelled, on the kitchen table
to be passed round and lit from below
and handed down. Leitz made this possible,
after one war and before another.
The best magnification, put your eye

as close as you can to the gentle tubes
of evaluation. My eyelashes
push hard against the lens (fall through, I thought
like Alice). Gentle action to the touch;
focus it then. I think it's not going to

happen like that again. If it's light years
away it's gone already. Layer
upon layer of body parts, failing
translucent skins like wet, dropping flowers,
old clothes, loose, decorative underwear.

Struggle, wriggle into those flowers now?
I'm in the front row. Near the head of the
queue. Do I like the price? It's on the hanger,
packaged nicely for sex; allure and swift
calculation. Like trying on an antique

camera for size, fitting lenses for
an eye test, seeing how to become a
crystal clear objective; finely severed
into slides of family history, juggling words
into the focus of today's lecture.

The displaying drawers were opened to
the light, then shut, clunk, like heavy picture
frames falling back against a wall. For good.
Gather round to hear the brain's fine lettering.
The microscope fits skin-tight in there. Sound.

Magnetic Resonance Imaging

i

Like going to the doctor for a figure of speech
to make things better, see things clearer. There
you'd be with a metaphor, like a cuddle,
some pain-relief to whisk you to sleep, through
the comforting hazy words, and out the other side
into a lovely world of images that easily stand
for nothing but themselves. Close your eyes to make
it large, larger, largest. Someone can see it
and put it on film, so like a picture, so like an echo
attracting and repelling across what you can only
imagine as noise in a vast cathedral dome, knocking
for a door, logged in your head, wordless.

ii

It's a microscope needed when the eyes
don't work or when the brain doesn't want to see,
and / or when it's become slowed down with
sloughed roughage, the paper and filings
off sharpened pencil ends. As though taking notes,
and rubbing them out; and more sketches,
and revising them for the future, was no longer
sensible. In the new picture it's all there:
the Poles, the Pole Star, visible magnetic
lines of force, singing, they might say as they
print it out, a resonant picture fixed
for life on the screen, banging into words
I heard. And I saw it, like a picture
from a satellite of the whole Earth's form,
so tiny, so flat, resolving the hard bits
of continental drift. Write it up, see.

In a standard folder with sealed notes:
it's a flop. Down to earth. To make something of it?
Tables. Cash it in for innumerable
mimetic patterns in the oceans or
my head. There you are. A prescription to count
it up and repeat it, repeat after
me. It's on paper and film now where the world ends:
allowed volcanic leakage, books of log tables,
plus or minus the numbers that aren't yet worth it.
But never mind, you might say, try harder, so:
not a pattern seen from a million miles
away, or even magnified colours through
a perfectly ground lens, softly bending light
onto my very own retina. Yet.
But work the science. There on celluloid,
a digital snap, counted out: left-overs,
change. Repeat. Times tables. Glowing solids.
If it grows too bright as it is then drug it.

Cast Adrift

'To the Centre of the Earth'
may have seemed a possible
journey when no one knew what
might be there. Now, inside, it's some
impenetrable, circling magnetic iron,
waiting to tipple its poles
from head to toe. Forces. Now you see them.
Lines of north and south distributed
through the upper worlds, to pass
into us, it might be said, like
a fraction of the world's soul.
Embodied. Nice idea. You can't stop
that one. Scribbled networks waiting to
be scanned, yes, read, and stilled
enough to be framed. Journey's end.
Store it up. Hang it on the wall
like a ship in a bottle
or a medical record. Now you don't.
But just feel for it now, with the taut,
meticulous rigging about to flower
into words for a second.
How would you read it? Blink. And then
hemp, flags, halyards, cables,
dried up fibres light up and seem
to burn, become nothing but trickling
unstoppable lava, red for danger. Scan
that. The lines of force must want it thus.
Read some more. Visible, there
on the surface; some atoms' as yet
unspoken grammar. Offer them
a subject, verb and object. Let it
lie for a second before you cast it.

Altamira

Finally things get underground. It's a whole lot
of work. For example, 'cave paintings'.
What can some space in another world,
below, have meant in some time now so obscured
through fancy labels? Quaternary, Magdalenian

footsteps overhead, underground, mine for the days
while polychromal chemicals last. Hold it: snap!
When we want some more energy we seem always
to mine it, dig for it. Carry our structures down.
And then set it on fire if it doesn't blow up

too soon. Or store it. And make pictures so safe that
no one can see them. Remember those silvery
leaf patterns exposed by chance on a slab of coal
waiting to go on the fire at home? It happened
in the brightness, and flickers away all that pressure,

finesse of hammered gold up in smoke
with old years, fossils and games. I still don't get it.
What we call paint or pigment gets brought
to what we call a cave. Or a safe or an archive,
perhaps. Somewhere for untold value to be securely held,

it's there, but it's not. Jewels, manuscripts, art,
food, bones from alien civilisations securely invisible
except where you want it most, in your head.
Can't see, won't see. But then again, eyes down,
I'm at the turnstile paying to enter the crypt,

or the gallery, the way to the stalactites like
spiders' webs, somewhere with a sabre tooth
stuck in the ceiling. I've still got to tick off
a coal mining museum and the Higgs Boson
accelerator. But I've done Killhope Wheel (lead),

Altamira and so many other sites. Down there,
where I've got it concealed and numbered,
is good enough for the most wonderful pictures.
Materials enough for brief, untimely illumination,
carried like figures to be added later in a complex sum,

carried away. What on earth did they do
when they came out from a day's painting
behind the scenes? Clean up? Scrub hands? Stained
clothes to wash? Shelve the rubbish to become
souvenirs? Lights fall out now. And you're in it.

Time Travel

Another Greek island holiday,
so at least one day in town buying
and looking. Relics heap up, so unplanned,
round any corner. Why do they
bother to dig any more? Why the cool,

clean display-cases indoors?
The guide-book says, 'For something
special go to the square and turn left
after the water tower.' Sure. Shade?
On steps to a closed door

rested a broken stone head
of a god, half there, half not.
The jaw smashed away
may have come from a sculptor's
final shot at beautification. I thought.

So shut out. Like queuing at a dentist's
office on a Sunday. Hopeless.
The museum was locked but pretty
and painful in the sunlight, set back
from today's street of bread

shops, postcards and refrigerators
and electric chandeliers. But the past
keeps popping up without photography
or spotlights. Snack on it. Bits lying
around like surgical waste and

used sharps in a future car boot sale.
How might it all get to market
to be a bargain memento
of how they suffered? No windows.
No security; it could all roll out.

Fingered. Well used. Tokens to exchange one
pain for another. If it's not the best
new stuff then it's 'Bring and Buy',
that's the American phrase. Nice one.
And we're all tourists wherever

we go or think. Whose words count?
'Seconds.' 'Sell out.' Do you
think it's all going to go? Not.
A half-finished memorial head
or torn up nerve-endings exposed

for all to see? What did the stone give
up so that we can look down on it
thus? We'll visit properly another time,
if ever. Dug up by accident and more
than part-cracked for somebody's profit.

Legacy perhaps; it's worth handing on,
passing down, passing by. What wonders,
one. What drill, was it, to pierce its eyeballs
for a pupil, stone-bled, rocky inner view
of the goods? A far-off retina dropped

on the pavement. Sad, so sad.
Cultures, now unreadable,
pile up, accumulate over our heads;
they will, with waste, throw-outs, bones,
shells and skin-dust, plastic bags of

dead excretion squeezed into tons
of evidence. It'll pile up, above it all.
So some chance dig finds my digital watch
and there it is as a topical gendered
decoration illuminated with great

dramatised interactive displays to
learn from. This talk's scum floating up there.
I'm looking up through it, page after page.
There are already thousands of years
waiting to search and turn it over. They

might be there scanning through any haphazard
earthenware library. To pass the time (listen
to that). Read me, speak to or for me. If
you please. Dentition. It's where it comes from.
You're up there and see what you see, I'm sure.

Enough. Broken jaw, worn teeth, see it
sometime at the end of a foul root canal.
Smell it out. I fear you might not want
to chew it over, at this point. Or would you?
There now. Spit in the bowl. Made it.

Sound Waves

For Michael Schmidt

A trip to the misericords in Manchester
is always worth it. For visiting relatives,
the kids on an off-day. Oddly hidden but
approachable. Or they were last time.

Cold, to be sure. And shiny, so felt-all-over,
so worn but touchable: a fox's head,
a peasant's nose to prop your backside on.
Unexpected centres of gravity

move from your stomach and down your legs
as you lean there. Just for a minute, a crude
version of standing still. What about hour after
hour? And days and years while so many

repeated waves of sound called out in long
notes, to smother, or soften, all talk of
pain. Taking up the time. Filling in the
space. Get through it or past it. Even the

echoes lap round your thinning leg muscles,
tuned to an old, falling pitch. Bandages
disposable, but so heartily
repeated to hold things in. The sound comes

round again if you wait. A form of ecstasy
for those bits of flesh. 'So, there now. Done?'
Touch and lean. Hour after hour. But not me.
Enough of charity. We're off. But the

ache is still there. Somehow the sound plasters
it over. Or paints it. What a composition!
A dressing that can change without hurting.
Waves of sound. Even so, imagine it

licking the stiff wood grain, resin, glass, grease
on your fingers. Taste them. Sexy. Shining
up the faces, clusters of grapes in precious
timber under the seat. Think of waiting

another hour before you permit it
to be personal again, to shift the
weight near to toppling the other way and
so near the floor. Stones. Near the future

and the future's future. Think that you won't
know how it'll be. No, you won't. Polish
it, wear it down. Smooth the stench away.
You never heard the sound stop. No, you didn't.

Carbon Holdings

Where is the combustion, now? Keeping it
inside. Fire-fighting boxed nicely blind in
hot metal, though there's lots of gas pumping
out. I want to put it somewhere for a
bit of a break. Secure holdings. Museum.

Like an underground car park. Such a great
idea – to hide our sacred transports
in something like a mineshaft. The tyres squeal
on rubber-shined curves. Like filmic alien screams.
Where's a free space? Going down and round again

to a deep powerhouse for all these electrics
and the lift from every circle. To somewhere.
There's a river close by up there, I guess,
next to level A. I'm not counting after
C. Car by car, nose-in to the concrete

and waterproof sides and steel props, and at
level H we've got a space. The floor spirals
on downwards. Racks of motors. Rules shine on
and off to prompt visitors like us, as
though in some sci-fi future-scape: switch off

engine, extinguish lights, report fires, no
smoking. Walking to the lift I think of
others: don't breath the carbon monoxide,
the carbon emissions, don't come back, just
leave it here. But not yet, I fear. Strangely,

you can almost squeeze the conditioned air,
this low, between your fingertips. Cleaned and
cooled, both dry and slimy. Rising through it,
the lift doors open in the sun. Get out.
Look round. Work, tours, coffee, art, whatever.

Get back. Down to earth, descending by swift
alphabetical levels as through a
mechanical substitute for the old
ways to die, returning into random
forms of carbon, it's all on offer in

adverts and diagrams, floor by floor, wall
by wall, bodies re-represented, lit
as value-added: stacked. This is the way
to acquire it and store it, in great tankers,
sealed in undersea pressure-holds for CO_2,

in well-secured tunnels for years to come,
for the stuff we've used and the stuff we want.
Diamonds, coal, graphite to draw with. Worth blood,
and more, if you say it's a jewel. The radio
said that the big thing for the next Mars

lander is to start digging. Makes sense. It'll
surely be nice down there, even an inch
or two. Dark, and irrecoverable.
It seems that all I can be is sorry
about it. And keep on driving. But I'm

not happy about 'sacred'. The word's too cheap,
too dear. A sort of tourism. Like this.
Dig in. Enjoy. Wait till it's clear. Swerve up,
squealing again, to the exit. Counted
out. Fill up quick, tank topped up, so safe.

Burnishing

BURNISHING, the Action of smoothing or polishing a Body, by violent rubbing it with any thing. Thus Book-binders *burnish* the Edges of their Books, by rubbing 'em with a Dog's Tooth. Gold and Silver are *burnish'd* with a Woolf's Tooth, or the bloody Stone, Tripoli, a piece of white Wood and Emery. Hence *Burnisher*, is a round polish'd piece of Steel, serving to smooth and give a Lustre to Metals: Of these there are various Kinds, of various Figures; straight, crooked, etc. Half *Burnishers*, are us'd to solder Silver, as well as to give it a Lustre.

Ephraim Chambers, *Cyclopaedia* 1728

Digitised Returns

Search engines discover innumerable
pasts, without being asked. Here's the offer
to send a copy of some census form or births,
marriages and death records that locate

our family names. And show identities
as either a shovel-maker in Worcester,
and then in Sheffield, or a penknife maker,
also in Sheffield. Choose. Which one's

family to follow backwards? It hardly matters
although they both shaped metal to cut. In.
Through. I wonder what. To lift coal or earth,
to heap or shift dung or night-soil. Nightly

and for always. Or writing accounts or
diaries, to sharpen a pencil before doing maths
in school or correcting something. I wonder
at the census details: so why want to know the

number of maidservants aged twelve, the sons
and daughters lined up along the terraced streets,
the occupations that forge and polish metal to its
brightest. And I wonder at 'finishers'. Always

turning things over, rolling things out, blowing
the sculpted shavings from a clean pencil-end,
skin and hair from a hollow cheek so it's shiny
and clean like a turned, brown furrow, ploughed

and cut up for more work. All that metal
to turn it over, soft and deep. To own
a well sprung penknife was a rite of passage,
to be able to do your own wood or paper

or cut your fingers deeply by accident –
that was power. Established. A way into
a family and a place in the tree. Metaphors,
all to make records (yes, you can think of

needles and wax before this stuff took over
the natural world of memory), hand-me-downs,
names of the next lot on the block, servants
of the written word to bash so sweetly

into a cutting edge. Leave them behind,
the lovely objects that stream out the ink.
Desire them so. It's a hidden wealth now.
Pocketable, a classless sharpener. Unopened.

Burnishing

To start with the words or start with the trade,
the action, offers something like philosophy.
To determine what 'burnisher' meant
in a page of Victorian census

data gets too easy. A fortune of serious
alternatives. I even find 'metal polishing
media'. So how would you give an account
of yourself? If you had to. Or if you could

choose the work. Or choose the name for what you do,
to put on, like spectacles for all to see.
Lenses and frames to decorate your face,
to make it all come close or far or green

or orange. Thus: 'And with this lens or this?
Is it clearer turned this way or like this?'
Brighter with tripoli? More transparent?
Agree with anything and it all comes clear

as though some correct words had tumbled out
of the dictionary, in the right order
and perfectly legible. Got it now.
Here is what they used to do on one street:

In 1861 – Back of Number 11,
file cutler and two scissor burnishers.
Back of Number 9, Butcher's tool steel grinder.
Number 9, Engineer's steel warehouseman

and two charwomen. Number 7, scissor forger cutler,
two scissor dresser cutlers. Home/Court,
Coal mine above surface labourer
and a table knife cutler. Number 5,

pocket knife blade grinder cutler, file cutler,
pocket knife blade grinder cutler,
table knife cutler. Six houses on this page.
Twenty-two women and girls, nine men and boys.

If they were at least 14 they were working.
Each was listed with a specific trade,
as you can read. But in another hand,
the specific words had been bracketed

and 'cutler' added to each. Easier
to add up the generality. These are
the names of the people at Number 5,
just another way of saying what they did

and who they were: Arthur, Priscilla, Nellie,
Robert, Martha and Lilly Glover.
Lilly was 8 and Martha 14. She worked
with table knives. No burnishers in that family.

The Census Form Poem

Reading the columns from left to right you start with 1,
'No. of Schedule', 2, 'ROAD, STREET &c, and No. or NAME
of HOUSE' [in Caps or lower case, like that], then whether or not
inhabited. Inhabited or uninhabited.

Like an island or colony, perhaps. 7, 'Number of rooms
if less than five'. Reading from right to left the first column
is 17, 'If (i) Deaf and Dumb (ii) Blind (iii) Lunatic
(iv) Imbecile, feeble-minded'. Column 16, 'WHERE BORN' [in Caps].

Column 15, 'If Working at Home', 14, 'Employer,
Worker, or Own Account', 13, 'PROFESSION OR OCCUPATION'
[in Caps]. It's funny that these columns are much wider than
8, 'Name and Surname of each person', and 9, 'RELATION

[in Caps] to Head of Family', 10, 'Condition as to Marriage',
and 11, 'Age last Birthday' of Males or Females. And all of these
must fit with an Administrative County, a Civil Parish,
an Ecclesiastical Parish, a County Borough,

Municipal Borough or Urban District, a ward of
Municipal Borough, or within an Urban District,
a Rural District, a Parliamentary Borough or District,
a Town or Village or Hamlet. Each House or Tenement,

including those with less than five rooms, was a 'Schedule'.
And at the bottom of the page is a 'NOTE [in Caps] –
Draw your pen through such words of the headings as are
inapplicable.' An imperative, to write out evidence of types

and ownership, location and possession. To ease the choice
of what to total up. In all, the one person who is addressed,
to have something to do, by those who designed the form,
announcing that he is good enough, is that man I allow myself

to see, who calls at each door. 'Draw your pen through
such words.' He will be trusted to know what sort you are.
And within which bounds and laws you were found.
I wonder which house he lived in, who counted him

and approved his inky gestures that record what he could
see inside, and then point out loud, as if in a schoolroom,
towards the names and wordless and senseless. He must
do things with words. It's an order. He's so lucky.

To each schedule he allocates its properties. Six people
in the three rooms at number 5. He gives them work or childhood.
I suppose a supervisor may have wanted them all as 'cutlers'.
Suits what's written. I wanted something of this to be what the

form might tell. But it's not stable; shifts like sand round a cold
casting lifted out. What have I found? At the top of the page
the big heading is, 'The under-mentioned Houses are situate
within the boundaries of the...' Just houses. And grammar.

Furnace Fires

For Marion Cassidy

I've just met someone who had seen from miles
away the steel city burn in 1940.
A spectacle, in a way, and unrepeatable.
Won't do that again. But imagine

losing your glasses in the wreck.
The street's gone. The way out's gone.
That'll teach you to learn what you've got
and not to think that way of seeing is

the end. Stuck tight in hot smoke and hot
metal. Crackling as though it were alive.
I'd rather delete the simile. The street
is acting to have a mind of its own.

Though from a distance, yes, it was a furnace,
a crucible or fire in hell that really was alive.
If I'd been locked in there how might I choose
some words to stop the pain? No substitutes.

I've seen the stored lists of families that
slept close together and walked in the dark
to the mills. Cast, or rolling metal out
for weapons. Or surgical instruments.

I've no idea what 1940 did
to their descendants. And I'm writing them
out again. Burnished, ground, dressed and framed;
I'm really sorry that I've done this.

Glimpse in the Furnace Shed

It's fire in the dark insides
and growing. But view only.
From a banked-up glow in one room
at home to the furnaces round

about. It's cold out there,
in the streets, the sheds,
stacks of coal that'll have
to heat up into coke,

into ash, into crude particle
stock. Doorways in, they're all
open tonight to feed more
men and oxygen towards

each scummy crucible. Make
steel pour out to the floor,
trickling light to show what's
known, and be what's known.

For seconds only
it's there for the asking
but slows to be solid and dull.
Give it here, press it, shape it

and work to bring back some
light, moments when metal
gets free and shiny, whatever's
in. No, can't say or write that.

So: 'in there', 'in its grey guts',
'in its visible, stainless innards
if it were broken across'. Joints
below skin deep, in metallic print.

Skin Filed for the Job

For so many ships and nails.
To make a handwritten list
into empirical stuff that can
be tested to breaking point

needs skin and nerves hardened up,
fit for purpose. The more
that's needed, the more gets
filed. Some desk jobs. Though they're

all adapted to shift for more metal
(would it crack or bend?), orders
apportioned to be sold on. And flesh
become so attached to it, mirror-like.

It's rock and ore easily liquid
in the half-light. Pulse. Shirt off.
Touch it. Tender for it. Though
beaten out so it'll weigh down

heavy. Is it a life? Its own thick
blood somewhere below the surface?
An image of their products
on their hands; same shape,

as solid as a medical model
replica in a visiting doctor's
office. On a shelf to illustrate
costed needs for the crusts of

power. Accidents and diseases.
Lungs will do. Cleft skin, grease it,
pick at it and worry it to keep
it hard and the cracks

as natural as any such disposable
surfaces on the hearth,
blast-furnace bottom, so close.
One more time, fingers

to the bone. Write that down along
the street. Shine it. Turning this
into anything to do with the hands
I used to see's an insult.

It's taken all my breath away.
No work, can't speak for coke, sand
and polish, casts for knives to see
your face in, and slag shoved out

and dumped to make more space.
Make room, make rooms.
To read and write in. Hot and cold.
I wonder at these jagged

surfaced bodies, cooked up. Made
up, I think. That's the way they
looked through the form, holding out
broken fingers, loving. Signed in.

1946 for Safe Keeping In

I have no idea why I still want this
to be preserved in any way. Then or now,
it's too like catching a ride. So what's left
of a man and woman we visited
after the war and after a tram ride?

Co-op tokens on the step to be explained.
A fireplace that was spotless, though the irons
were only shiny where they must be held.
We all had those, the same love of heat
and what could make it. A house and its smell

that was so unknowable, solid green
soap, washing in and out. I'll try to respect
that memory. (Don't complain. I'm answering
you already.) Go back. Prepare it as
though to be stored in acid-free folders

in air-conditioned archives. Catalogue it?
Links in the web as something with potential
meaning? Joined up. But it won't lie down, see.
I probably only saw him when he
came home and was cleaned up. But his hands

stayed worn from the steel-pouring ladles.
I knew, no, I saw that. As a child
I watched his thick-skinned fingers carrying
tea-cups, and, stiffly holding the pot;
he felt no heat from the long-mashed tea.

'Worn', you see, like that. I am trying not
to describe him or write anything that
would soften that terrible, cracked skin or
rescue it from the blaze to be preserved,
cells all caked-up and darkened for protection

to be usefully near old ore or coke.
Breathing, too, I saw and heard (learn it)
as accountable to manufacture,
to industry; so long as you could still
cough and carry weight, that work could be owned,

I suppose, by someone. For the wages
bill, for the pay-packet, for the perfectly
cut and buttered bread and raspberry jam,
the tea still hot, the clock chiming again
at quarter past. Even then I might have

thought such singing, repeating metal notes
an odd match for the hands that could still just
wind the springs, finger tips of printless cells
splitting and joining, to fill up space, and
perform what nature wants to win the war.

They're immune, or devouring each other,
lumping up with single-celled floating
bacteria eased out for you to see
or use, it's not all waste. But I really
want to hear that cough, again, ring like the

most beautiful music that is nothing
to do with the paper it's written on.
It's not for you, or you. Or anyone.
Embedded in employment files to be
numbered might be all; safe from this, but praised.

Postscript

Seeing As

Many years ago when I was a student of philosophy I wondered at some of the questions which engaged us. Where or what was the present King of France? Where or what was a minus number, or, indeed, the number three? If 'this' is good where or what is the goodness in 'this'? I remember a sense that they often 'clicked', as though someone or something had turned a switch, audibly, in my head so that a question made sense and was complete in itself. Just as a particular note in a piece of music was both itself and a part of a melody that had come from somewhere and was going somewhere, like a point on a curve, so seeing Wittgenstein's simple drawing as a duck or a rabbit seemed a perfect and complete experience. Similarly, to see black squares on white, or white squares on black, could be 'done' there and then, it was in my power, in anyone's power. Surely?

Part of Wittgenstein's thinking which stayed with me from the early 1960s concerned 'seeing as'. The mystery, and accompanying pleasure of seeing things anew, was good enough:

> The change of aspect. 'But surely you would say that the picture is altogether different now!'
> But what is different: my impression? my point of view? – Can I say? I *describe* the alteration like a perception; quite as if the object had altered before my eyes.
>
> (Wittgenstein, *Philosophical Investigations*,
> Oxford 1963, p. 195e)

I have no idea whether philosophers still find this worthy of study. But I found that it fitted perfectly with the experience of reading, 'Shall I compare thee…?' and being excited by the Metaphysicals. I also felt the intensity of the debate about imagery and comparison as it moved from Pope to Johnson and on to Wordsworth: the image chosen or chosen for you changed the world:

> 'Is it a *genuine* visual experience?' The question is: in what sense is it one?

Here it is *difficult* to see that what is at issue is the fixing of concepts.

A *concept* forces itself on one. (This is what you must not forget.)

For when should I call it a mere case of knowing, not seeing? – Perhaps when someone treats the picture as a working drawing, *reads* it like a blueprint. (Fine shades of behaviour. – Why are they *important*? They have important consequences.)

(Wittgenstein, *Philosophical Investigations*, Oxford 1963, p. 204e)

Here, Wittgenstein recognises the strange interrelations between 'knowing', 'seeing', 'experiencing', 'seeing as', 'conceptualising', and 'behaving'. I suppose that what attracted me to lines like these was their similarity to poetry, in that they assumed that, as you thought and spoke them, there were immediate questions and consequences; the thought-processes were active as they went along and never final. The questions were more important than any answers.

The lack of answers in some of the experiences of being diagnosed with MS seemed to fit what I wanted to write. A lot of it had all the paradox of being complete and memorable (that half hour in the scanner; those minutes of the spinal tap; reading and re-reading that helpful leaflet). But none of it had answers. I remember very clearly lying in the MRI machine being fascinated by what it was 'seeing' and 'seeing as' in my brain; wanting to have the power to know, to conceptualise and to read it 'like a blueprint'. 'Fine shades of behaviour' indeed. The duck-rabbit was not part of the means of diagnosis but, amazingly, the black and white squares were. Imagine a computer screen with the squares of a chessboard switching from black to white and black to white incessantly. It is a standard method of discovering how quickly the messages get from each eye to the brain. Would a philosopher like the term 'visually evoked potentials'? After ten minutes seeing through one eye only, and then the other, it made me sleepy.

Jean-Martin Charcot, the nineteenth-century neurologist who 'framed' MS, and with whom Freud studied, might have enjoyed 'seeing as' in an MRI scanner rather than having to dissect plaques (sclerosis) from nerve fibres:

[Charcot] was heard to say that the greatest satisfaction man can experience is to see something new, that is, to recognise it as new, and he constantly returned with repeated observations to the subject of the difficulties and the value of such 'seeing'. He wondered how it happened that in the practice of medicine men could only see what they had been taught to see; he described how wonderful it was suddenly to see new things – new diseases – though they were probably as old as the human race; he said that he had to admit that he could now see many a thing which for thirty years in his wards he had ignored.

(Sigmund Freud, quoted in T. Jock Murray,
Multiple Sclerosis: The History of a Disease, New York 2005)

Scanners, microscopes, telescopes, the seventeen-mile circular Large Hadron Collider tube at CERN (the Conseil Européen pour la Recherche Nucléaire near Geneva) all seem to mediate our ways of seeing. We seem to like images 'yoked by violence together'. I wonder.

Being slid into the narrow scanner tube surrounded by powerful, noisy magnets was not immediately 'poetic'; it alters the direction of the body's hydrogen atoms' magnetic field. They emit different radio waves which can be scanned:

Different tissues emit different signals; for example water (e.g. cerebrospinal fluid) appears white while fatty tissues (e.g. brain) appear darker. Diseased tissues often have a higher water content than the surrounding tissues and so appear lighter in colour on the scan. This is the case with plaques in MS which appear white.

(Megan Burgess, *Multiple Sclerosis: Theory & Practice for Nurses*,
London 2002)

So there were the tell-tale images. As they say, a diagnosis was 'suggested'. And for me it was a strange way to become a student again, to see the resonances. But the way in which the power of the giant magnets at CERN and those nearer to home came together in the poems was far more indirect and odd than the kind and clear interpretation of my condition given by Megan Burgess in 2004. It led to a strenuous exploration of analogies revealed through physical processes of science and then on to another totally unpredicted mimetic link between my callous sense of family history and metal-work in 'Burnishing'; a reconciling at least, if not 'uniting in harmony'.

Geoffrey Hill, whose lectures I attended in 1962 and whom I heard reading his poems soon after, says in 'Poetry as "Menace" and "Atonement"' that 'the technical perfecting of a poem is an act of atonement', an experience described by Yeats when he wrote that 'a poem comes right with a click like a closing box'. On reflection, I hope that some of the poems in *Magnetic Resonance Imaging* have created an at-one-ment through an unpredictable 'click like a closing box', seeing (seeing as?) knowable and un-knowable worlds: to scan to a strange mimesis.